LIFE-CHANGING ADVENTURE

Copyright © 2021 by Emma Huffam and Trevor Builder

First published in 2021 by Cut Lunch Adventures
www.cutlunchadventures.com

ISBN: 978-0-6453041-0-7
Paperback Edition

All rights reserved. No part of this publication may be reproduced, stored in a retrieval system, copied in any form or by any means, electronic, mechanical, photocopying, recording or otherwise transmitted without written permission from the authors. You must not circulate this book in any format.

The right of Emma Huffam and Trevor Builder to be identified as authors of this Work has been asserted by them in accordance with sections 77 and 78 of the Copyright, Designs and Patents Act 1988.

This book is based on the authors' experiences and is designed to provide inspiration and motivation for our readers. The content of this book is only the expression and opinion of the authors. Outdoor adventure can be dangerous - you are responsible for your own safety. Although the authors and publisher have taken all reasonable care in preparing this book, we make no warranty about the accuracy or completeness of its content and, to the maximum extent permitted, disclaim all liability from its use.

Life-Changing Adventure

Be daring, be inspired. Adventure is waiting for you.

EMMA HUFFAM AND TREVOR BUILDER

www.cutlunchadventures.com

To our families for their life-long inspiration and support.

CONTENTS

Introduction

LIFE-CHANGING ADVENTURE

DISCOVER

1 - Discover What You're Capable Of

2 - Discover Your Perseverance

3 - Discover Your Strength

4 - Discover Your Resilience

5 - Discover Your Power

COURAGE

6 - Courage To Face Adversity

7 - Courage To Face Isolation

8 - Courage To Face A Challenge

9 - Courage To Face Your Fear

10 - Courage To Face Uncertainty

EXPERIENCE

11 - Experience Awe

12 - Experience Freedom

13 - Experience Simplicity

14 - Experience Balance

15 - Experience Joy

ADVENTURE AWAITS

Acknowledgements

About the Authors

INTRODUCTION

The concept of a life-changing adventure is often a mystery. People who have returned from adventures say that something changed inside them, but they couldn't describe it.

Through this book, we explore the concept of life-changing adventures with you.

- What can you discover about yourself?

- What courage do you need?

- What can you experience?

We ask you thought-provoking questions to encourage you to consider your perspective. Perhaps you can recall similar experiences in your own life. We also provide extracts from our adventure blog as examples.

We hope this book inspires you, gets you thinking and motivates you to plan your next adventure.

LIFE-CHANGING ADVENTURE

Adventures of any kind may change your life in some way. You could be moving house, starting a new job or exploring the world. Whatever adventure you have, you will learn something from it.

An outdoor adventure offers you the possibility of a life-changing experience, especially if you're willing to take on a big challenge like trekking in the Himalayas, which is what we did.

Although this book includes examples of trekking, it also applies to other outdoor adventures, especially those in the mountains and those with a challenge.

Why Adventure?

There are a variety of reasons why people choose to go on a challenging adventure. Sometimes people are motivated by life events - for example, milestone birthdays or a need to get away from the everyday grind.

Some people seek a new challenge or goal. Others would like to escape to the wilderness, take in the spectacular scenery and gain a fresh perspective.

The Complete Adventure Experience

The moment you sign up for a big adventure, you feel an incredible sense of anticipation. Not long after, this is followed by trepidation as it begins to sink in what you're taking on!

A trek, for example, is more than just the trek itself. It's an absorbing personal project that you become immersed in over many months. The whole experience is invigorating. It includes the time you spend planning, preparing, training and taking part. On your return, there is recovery and reflection. The effects have a lasting impact.

Adventure in the Mountains

For us, one of the most life-changing experiences was our first trek in the Himalayas to Everest Base Camp. We had a physical, mental and spiritual experience rolled into one. We returned home with a renewed sense of perspective.

Since then, we have embarked on a new trajectory in life - with our lifestyle, trekking and our adventure website.

Adventures allow you to grow and the mountains always have something to teach you.

Your Inner Self

Life-changing adventures have an element of self-discovery. Daring to venture outside your comfort zone, you can discover just how capable you are. As a result, you must dig deep. You return with new insights and experiences. They have a profound impact on you.

You gain confidence and perhaps a renewed sense of purpose. You meet like-minded people as you explore a new world of adventure.

The experience awakens your senses as well as your emotions. And it might even touch you spiritually. You may be more grounded and connected with the universe. In the Himalayas, we found the Sherpa culture combined with the mountains created a powerful yet calming place to be - the here and now.

You can find it an all-consuming personal experience. To survive, you need to practice self-care and put yourself first for a change. You appreciate the small comforts.

You find a creative, contemplative experience that can only happen when distanced from your day-to-day life, with little or no communication to the outside world. You immerse yourself in the new surroundings. Having time to think, you're able to solve problems, stimulate ideas and gain insights.

You find yourself in the stillness of the present moment. All your energies focus on the task at hand, you're 'in the zone' – the state of flow - and you're invincible.

You have the freedom to be your real authentic self. What others think of you doesn't matter out here.

Lasting Impacts

Life-changing adventures also stay with you for years afterward. Never fading into oblivion as a sightseeing holiday might do.

They have a profound impact. You come back thinking differently, which can lead to other changes in your life.

You want to stay connected to your experience. Perhaps you share your stories with other like-minded adventurers. You may like to read books or watch films about adventure. It may even inspire you to follow the adventures of others.

Naturally, there is a recovery period after an adventure. You may even experience the post-adventure blues, as you miss the magical mystery world that has been your home for the past days, weeks, even months.

However, something has changed inside. A switch has flicked, and new ideas have sparked. Hopefully, you are fulfilled and satisfied by your accomplishment. You become motivated again, uplifted. At the least, it will have been a valuable learning experience, equipping you for future challenges in life.

People who have returned from a life-changing adventure have a knowing look about them. As though they have come face to face with the essence of who they are.

There might even be a sense of pilgrimage or transformation since they had to go on an outer journey to discover what they already knew inside. The experience is intense and enriching.

But the story doesn't end there. One adventure leads to another, and there's always the next one to plan.

What Do You Think?

- What's your definition of adventure?

- Which natural outdoor environments have the most impact on you?

- What led to the most significant turning points in your life?

DISCOVER

1 - Discover What You're Capable Of

You can discover what you're capable of when you set yourself a challenge and go on an adventure.

Try something new, go somewhere different or step up to the next level. You might surprise yourself with what you can achieve.

Trekking in the Himalayas is a perfect example. Test yourself on a 2-3 week expedition at high altitude. See the world's highest mountains while immersing yourself in the local culture.

It is a life-changing adventure, challenging you both physically and mentally. It has a profound effect on you and gives you the appetite and confidence to go on and do more.

WHAT DO YOU THINK?

Have you ever surprised yourself with what you've been able to achieve?

Is there something you'd like to prove to yourself that you can do?

Do you have the appetite for a new challenge?

"Several years ago began a remarkable journey into the Himalayas culminating in our first trek to Everest Base Camp. To fall in love with the Himalayas is a dream come true. Ordinary people, doing extraordinary things."

EVEREST BASE CAMP TREK
NEPAL

2 - Discover Your Perseverance

You can discover your perseverance when you set yourself a challenge and go on an adventure.

Sometimes you surprise yourself at how good you are at persevering when you want something. Motivation is often the underlying factor in whether you're successful or not.

You might need to persevere when it's a particularly hard or lengthy challenge. You'll need to draw on your physical and mental resources and perhaps seek help from others.

There is a great feeling of triumph and achievement if you can persevere and reach your goal.

Just put one foot in front of the other. One step at a time - and discover your perseverance!

WHAT DO YOU THINK?

When have you shown your perseverance to complete a difficult task or challenge?

What motivated you to continue? What did you say to yourself?

Did you surprise yourself with what you were able to achieve?

_____

_____

_____

_____

_____

_____

_____

"Encountering unseasonably deep snow higher up added to the challenging trek. Our guides did a great job of navigating the path and breaking trail. With a clear focus on each step, looking up occasionally for the views, we had a steely determination to get to our next camp."

MAKALU ADVANCE BASE CAMP TREK
NEPAL

3 - Discover Your Strength

You discover your strength when you set yourself a physical challenge in the outdoors.

There's nothing like a physical challenge, such as a multi-day trek, to lull you out of your routine. That moment when you grasp what you've just signed up for. How fit and strong will you have to be? What else do you need to prepare? It will require mental strength as well.

You may be surprised by your strength and how much you have. Completing an outdoor challenge where you have given it your all and achieved your goal is also very satisfying.

WHAT DO YOU THINK?

What has required you to call on your strength the most?

How much of it was a physical vs mental challenge?

What's your next physical challenge going to be?

_____

_____

_____

_____

_____

_____

_____

"At one stage, I must admit I had contemplated turning back. I'm so glad though, that I found that inner strength inside of me and pushed on."

TEN PEAKS TREK - KOSCIUSZKO NATIONAL PARK
AUSTRALIA

4 - Discover Your Resilience

You discover your resilience on an outdoor adventure.

Sometimes the big things test you, and other times an accumulation of small things. What is the tipping point at which you make that decision to give up or carry on? What do you draw on to bounce back and keep going – is it what you tell yourself, or do you rely on encouragement from others? How do you motivate others through their challenges?

It might surprise some, but an outdoor adventure is more of a mental challenge than a physical one. You need to draw on your inner strength to be able to tackle difficult situations as they arise.

Whether you succeed or not in your adventure goal, you will always return home with valuable insights. Perhaps you surprise yourself with how well you coped. Other times you may have had hard lessons which shook you to your core. Either way, you are richer for the experience.

We learned a lot from the treks that did not go so well. We tackled challenging terrain, bad weather and high altitude. Sometimes we struggled through illness and injury or coped with living conditions that were less than ideal.

It's funny how sometimes the most challenging experiences are the ones that teach you the most and help you go on to achieve bigger and better things. Your resilience grows throughout life.

> "As it turned out, we weren't as nearly 'mentally' prepared as we thought we were."
>
> MERA PEAK EXPEDITION
> NEPAL

> "Climbing up, pretty much exhausted, I didn't come all this way to give up now!"
>
> MT TARANAKI
> NEW ZEALAND

WHAT DO YOU THINK?

How do you cope when you have setbacks and things do not go to plan?

What helps you bounce back and motivates you to keep going?

What would you tell yourself next time you're thinking about giving up?

5 - Discover Your Power

You discover your power when you immerse yourself in the outdoors on an adventure.

Choosing to go on an adventure is empowering in itself. Committing to a big goal is your choice. You're deciding to set yourself a challenge and try something new.

In the presence of an 8,000m mountain or a raging river, you may feel small or insignificant. However, you can marvel at nature's power and draw strength from it at the same time. When you're in the present moment, you feel invincible.

Having the power to survive in the wilderness or unknown places can teach you a lot about yourself. Sometimes you need to dig deep to find those reserves of physical or mental strength that you weren't aware you had.

Upon facing the power of nature, such as gazing up at large mountains, you might even feel a connection. Something that stirs the spirit and speaks to your core. That gives you insight into the power you've always had.

WHAT DO YOU THINK?

Where or when do you feel the most empowered?

What impact does the power of nature have on your emotions, especially when you're in amongst it?

What's your next personal project going to be?

_____

_____

_____

_____

_____

_____

_____

"Reaching an altitude of some 5,800m/ 19,028ft, this trek was definitely not for the faint-hearted. It's the highest altitude that we've trekked to date. Coupled with the weather, the landscape up high was very stark, consisting of rocky and snowy terrain."

CHO OYU ADVANCE BASE CAMP TREK
TIBET, CHINA

COURAGE

6 - Courage to Face Adversity

Going on an adventure can sometimes test your courage in facing adversity. Sometimes you have a choice, and at other times not. Depending on your perspective, the level of difficulty or unpleasantness of the situation could be different.

Signing up for an adventure usually means you are up for some element of risk. But of course, that provides an opportunity to discover what you are capable of.

It is possible to anticipate and prepare for many types of adversity. For example, you could expect wild weather, high altitude and challenging living conditions.

On the other hand, you may end up in situations that you did not foresee. These test your courage and ability to manage the challenge that is facing you.

Either way, you have to make decisions when you face adversity – what do you do? Do you persevere, or do you give up? Perhaps you have no option but to go on. What do you need to do to survive? Or to be safe and to get through the challenge? What are you capable of, physically and mentally?

There are certainly benefits in mustering the courage to face adversity, providing that you live to tell the tale! You always learn something, and there's the satisfaction of having achieved your objective. The belief and confidence that you gain in yourself will help in future situations throughout life. You also return with more appreciation of the good things in life.

> "Finishing in the darkness, we fell into the refugio somewhat weather-beaten, but with spirits intact. Along with the freezing conditions, snow blowing from every conceivable angle you could imagine and a few 'motivating' words to the group – all set the tone for the rest of the trip."
>
> PYRENEES ALPINE ADVENTURE
> FRANCE AND SPAIN

WHAT DO YOU THINK?

What challenges in life have taught you the most?

How much does facing adversity add to, rather than dull, your sense of achievement?

How do you motivate yourself to tackle challenges when faced with them?

_____

_____

_____

_____

_____

_____

_____

7 - Courage to Face Isolation

Going on an adventure can sometimes test your courage to face isolation. Your physical and mental resources need to be up to the task.

Being in remote locations with limited or no communications with the rest of the world can be scary. It can also be liberating.

Having to rely on your resources, limited to what you brought with you, brings things into sharp reality – you can't just pop down to the local store or order online. You need to call on your ingenuity and creativity to solve any problems you encounter.

Being isolated also means not being up to date with the latest things happening in the world. On the flip side, you're treated to the solitude of peace and quiet.

So do you have the courage to face isolation?

WHAT DO YOU THINK?

Where is the most remote place you've been? How was the experience?

What elements of isolation did you like or dislike?

What creative solutions have you come up with in the past when solving a problem with limited resources?

"The opportunity provided us with a traverse of Patagonia, travelling its length from north to south. The majority of which was done on foot, some by bus and other by boat via some of the most captivating and untouched national parks in the region."

GREAT PATAGONIAN TRAVERSE
CHILE AND ARGENTINA

8 - Courage to Face a Challenge

An adventure tests your courage to face a challenge. You never quite know what's going to happen, and that's what gives it the edge. Your senses awake and there's a spark of excitement as you go outside of your comfort zone.

Of course, there's the initial challenge of taking on the adventure in the first place. But then you'll no doubt face challenges along the way – some which you can anticipate and others which throw up surprises.

Whatever happens, you always learn something about yourself in the process. You might take away valuable lessons about what you'd do differently next time. And the bonus is that you come away having extended yourself and your comfort zone. Who knows how, in the future, that extra grit you discovered is going to help you out.

So do you have the courage to face a challenge and to push yourself? Maybe all you need is a nudge. Or perhaps a shove. Whatever the case, don't scuttle your dreams by any self-imposed limitations about what you can or cannot do.

WHAT DO YOU THINK?

Do you drive yourself to take on new challenges? Or are you more influenced by others?

In the past, how have you extended your comfort zone?

Is the idea of a new adventure exciting to you?

_____

_____

_____

_____

_____

_____

_____

"The trek itself was hard going but definitely rewarding. Scrambling over rocks, dodging rock slides and a frozen river was all in a day's work."

KANCHENJUNGA NORTH/SOUTH BASE CAMP TREK
NEPAL

9 - Courage to Face Fear

Being on an adventure tests your courage to face fear.

The fact that adventure involves you doing something new means that somehow you are stepping outside your comfort zone. When you comprehend what you have committed to, an awkward moment of panic can then follow the euphoria of joining an exciting adventure.

Fear not, as it's probably a good thing that your panic highlights the preparation that you will need to do. Perhaps it's your fitness, your mental strength, your gear, your skills or your knowledge of what you'll be facing. Your confidence will grow the more you prepare.

But there's always that nagging doubt or question in your mind. How risky is it? Am I good enough? Uncertainty is the nature of adventure. Isn't that what made it exciting in the first place?

You can turn that vulnerability from a weakness into a strength. Acknowledge your fears and do your best to mitigate the risks. Once on the trail, manage fears as best you can. Many fears may not even come to fruition. Have the courage to face your fear.

WHAT DO YOU THINK?

How have you overcome fear before?

What would you fear on an outdoor adventure?

Would that stop you from going?

_____

_____

_____

_____

_____

_____

_____

"We were about to set off, when we came upon a sign on the National Park Notice Board – 'WARNING: there have been sightings of a mother grizzly bear and her cub in the area. Strongly recommend hiking in groups of four or more people.'"

LARCH VALLEY / SENTINEL PASS
BANFF NATIONAL PARK, CANADA

10 - Courage to Face Uncertainty

Going on an adventure tests your courage to face uncertainty.

Any adventure has some level of uncertainty, given it's something new you're doing. There's always something different or unknown about what you could experience.

You can't be a control freak in the mountains or any natural environment when nature has the upper hand. While you can plan for possible eventualities, you are still never 100% certain what will happen. The weather, the trail conditions, altitude, your team - the obstacles you might face can vary. It helps to be comfortable when facing uncertainty.

Uncertainty is also part of the everyday world where things can go wrong, such as lost baggage and flight delays.

However, on the flip side, uncertainty can also mean discovering pleasant surprises along the way. No matter how much you've read up on the adventure beforehand, you still never know what it will be like once you get there.

So how can you be comfortable with uncertainty? While you can plan and prepare, you also need to be flexible. It helps to be resilient and adaptable to change. If you can let go and see what happens, then the adventure will surely be more enjoyable. Tackle each day as it comes – the here and now. And you'll come back with some good stories to tell!

> "One of the experiences of trekking in the Himalayas, aside from some of the best mountain views in the world, is that you never know what to expect. From snow and ice one day, to sunshine the next."

ANNAPURNA DHAULAGIRI TREK
NEPAL

WHAT DO YOU THINK?

How comfortable are you with ambiguity, vagueness, uncertainty?

How willing are you to try new things and experiences?

What's something different you could try today?

_____

_____

_____

_____

_____

_____

_____

EXPERIENCE

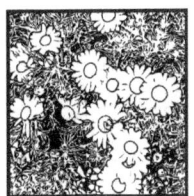

11 - Experience Awe

Experience awe when you go on an adventure in the mountains.

How do you describe that feeling of being taken aback and touched to your core when you witness a sight that is beyond beautiful? Sublime, some would say.

It's a funny word, awe, especially when describing everything in the context of being 'awesome'. We also tend to repeat other words when describing mountain scenery. For example, spectacular, breathtaking, amazing, awe-inspiring and majestic. So what does it mean for a person to be awestruck?

There are many beautiful places in the natural world. But there is something different about certain mountains that take your breath away. They brighten your day and leave a lasting impression on you.

It's hard to describe the feeling. Sometimes the view will be startling as you round a corner and there it is. Such a grand sight of a mountain on a giant scale rising far into the sky. It's dramatic, astounding, unbelievable.

Perhaps you are fortunate to see a sweeping panorama of beauty on a clear day that brings tears to your eyes.

Sometimes it may be the state of mind you're in that day. The mountain appears, and it's just what you need. It moves you deeply in some way.

> "We climbed to the top of Gokyo Ri (5,483m / 17,988ft). Views of Cho Oyu, Everest, Nuptse and Lhotse with Makalu in the background. Words cannot describe the beauty of the Himalayas!"

EVEREST CIRCUIT AND CHO LA PASS
NEPAL

WHAT DO YOU THINK?

Have you experienced awe from a beautiful sight?

What makes it different compared with anything else you've seen?

Which sights or scenes have made a lasting impression on you?

_____

_____

_____

_____

_____

_____

_____

12 - Experience Freedom

Experience the freedom to be yourself when you go on an adventure.

In the wilderness, you are free from the hustle and bustle of the world. You escape emails, phone calls, to-do lists, demands, expectations and the daily grind. You can disconnect from the news and social media you receive each day.

Being in the wilderness also necessitates a focus on your basic survival needs. You can be the real raw 'you' instead of hiding behind the layers that the world sees. No need for job titles, egos, work clothes or makeup. No chance to have the perfect hairstyle. There is no point in hiding your thoughts and feelings if they're going to help you survive. You are free to reveal your vulnerabilities.

Just being in nature or the mountains will free your spirit.

WHAT DO YOU THINK?

At what times or places have you experienced a great sense of freedom?

When do you feel the least free?

When do you think that you are most 'yourself'?

"Hooking up with a 'flying beaver' (float plane), we headed out over a remote ice field into a pristine lake environment where we were dropped off for four days of isolation."

CARIBOO CHILCOTIN COAST MOUNTAINS
BRITISH COLUMBIA, CANADA

13 - Experience Simplicity

Experience the simplicity of life when you go on an adventure.

Being around nature connects you to the world and has a grounding effect on you. It might be amongst forests, mountains, desert or coastline. Life is at its simplest and most basic. There are no city high-rises, traffic jams and complexities of modern life.

Your only focus is the environment around you, the weather and just having to eat, walk and sleep. Your mind is free of clutter and is allowed to wander. You get lost in the pleasant moments of being outdoors. Even in bad weather, when occupied with getting to your destination safely, you can still enjoy nature at its most dramatic.

On an adventure, you get to experience simplicity in the way you live too. Your meals consist only of the food you can carry or what's available. You're typically sleeping in basic accommodation - whether it's a tent, hut or teahouse. The gear you take with you is limited to what you need and what can be carried.

There are fewer decisions to make - such as what to wear, what to eat and what to do today. You appreciate the simple things in life even more. Imagine a nice warm cup of tea or hot chocolate after a day out hiking in cold weather. Imagine how much more you appreciate a hot shower after days or weeks on the trail.

> "Dining al fresco, with the stars shining ever so brightly in the sky above us, we fell asleep content with how the day unfolded. Looking up at the clear night sky and sighting the Southern Cross along with other constellations was a sight to behold."

JAGUNGAL WILDERNESS
AUSTRALIA

WHAT DO YOU THINK?

When do you experience simplicity at its best?

What needs simplifying in your daily life?

Where are the nicest places in nature near you?

14 - Experience Balance

Experience balance of mind, body and soul when you go on an adventure in the natural world.

Your daily life at home may be mentally demanding some days and physically demanding on others. Escaping from routine, especially from the city and modern life, can help bring you back to the real world. You feel more connected, more grounded when you're out in nature.

An adventure, such as a hike or trek, also requires you to use your mind and body in a more focussed way to help you reach your goal for the day. Being in the moment or natural environment can also be spiritually uplifting.

You may also experience balance across all your senses through your surroundings. Perhaps the sight of beautiful scenery lifts your spirit. Listen to sounds of streams and rivers, the wind and any animals or birds. Notice the different smells around you. Taste the food you eat on the trail, which you savour when hungry. Feel the elements on your skin – the strong breeze, the hot sun, the cold snow.

While trekking in places like the Khumbu region of the Himalayas in Nepal, there is a spiritual element to be found.

Passing through villages, you experience the peaceful Sherpa culture and their respect for the mountains. For good luck, you spin the prayer wheels and walk clockwise around mani (prayer) walls and stupas. You appreciate the fluttering prayer flags and fragrant incense. You experience a feeling of connection with the mountains.

It inspires a sense of balance and calm.

> "In this remote part of the island, we were treated to pure white sand beaches and sparkling turquoise seas, waves crashing on the intense orange granite boulders."
>
> BAY OF FIRES TREK
> TASMANIA, AUSTRALIA

> "After winding through vivid green native forest, the track burst out onto a sun-drenched beach with golden sands and crystal-clear water."
>
> ABEL TASMAN COAST TRACK
> NEW ZEALAND

WHAT DO YOU THINK?

How balanced is your daily life?

Where or when have you experienced the feeling of being in balance?

Where do you like going to enjoy peace and quiet?

_____

_____

_____

_____

_____

_____

_____

15 - Experience Joy

Experience a sense of joy when you go on an adventure in the natural world, especially on a trek or hike.

You can find joy just from what you observe. It could be beautiful scenery such as mountains and rivers, forests or wildflowers. You might be lucky to spot wild animals and birds. Experiencing different cultures and meeting locals along the way also enhances your trek.

You may find joy in simple, perhaps unexpected, things that you take for granted at home. Imagine the pleasure of eating a much-needed snack on the trail or a hot meal after a long hard day.

Happiness and joy may come simply from being underway on the trail and feeling alive. By focussing your physical, mental and spiritual energies on the task at hand. The simple process of walking and navigating obstacles. The pleasure of breathing in the fresh air on a sunny day, feeling the breeze on your face.

Sometimes you experience joy when you emerge into a different area, such as trekking above the tree line. Suddenly the views are expansive and the alpine environment has an uplifting effect on you. Or it's the time of day – seeing the mountains silhouetted against the sunrise or sunset. Perhaps the season makes the difference – the shades of autumn, the bright summer sunlight, the stillness of winter, the freshness of spring.

Ultimately upon completing your trek or even reaching milestones along the way, you experience the joy of achieving your goal (and a hot shower!!). You can also re-live that joy in your photos and memories afterward.

> "The best Great Walk in New Zealand. The variety of landscapes were a joy to walk through: mountains reaching into the sky; deep sweeping valleys; pure lakes and waterfalls; lush beech forests."

ROUTEBURN TRACK
NEW ZEALAND

WHAT DO YOU THINK?

What brings you joy in the outdoors?

Is it the big or small things? Is it what you see or what you experience?

Which achievements have given you the most joy?

_____

_____

_____

_____

_____

_____

_____

ADVENTURE AWAITS

Are the mountains calling?

Is it time to plan your next adventure?

Be daring!

ACKNOWLEDGEMENTS

We're deeply grateful to so many people for encouraging, helping and supporting us on the adventures which have inspired this book.

At home, our families, friends and fitness trainers keep us motivated. On the trails, our fellow adventurers, trekking guides and crew provide great company and support. Online, we are inspired by following the adventures of mountaineers, trekkers and many others - some who we've had the pleasure of walking with on the trails.

Special thanks to Sarah for helping us to proofread this book.

Thank you to all of you.

Emma and Trevor

 New Zealand-born Emma and Australian-born Trevor are avid adventurers based in Sydney, Australia. They love to trek. When not at home they are often found on a trekking adventure somewhere in the Himalayas, New Zealand or Australia.

In 2013 they set themselves a big challenge of trekking to Everest Base Camp, inspired by the opportunity to celebrate the 60th anniversary of the first ascent of Mt Everest, with fellow adventurers and climbers.

Once in Nepal, they were immersed in an exhilarating culture and were awestruck by the highest mountains in the world. They became captivated by the whole experience that trekking offers: challenging goals, physical and mental fitness and a vibrant community. A life-changing experience.

Since then, they have completed many treks worldwide and now publish online adventure resources for trekkers. They love to encourage people on their own adventures in life.

Project Base8000 is their latest challenge. The goal is to trek to the base camps of the world's 14 highest mountains over 8000m.

In the community, Emma and Trevor support the Australian Himalayan Foundation.

You can visit their websites at:

www.cutlunchadventures.com

www.projectbase8000.com

www.australianhimalayanfoundation.org.au

www.ingramcontent.com/pod-product-compliance
Lightning Source LLC
Chambersburg PA
CBHW070311010526
44107CB00056B/2560